BYE-BYE
LAND

THE ISABELLA GARDNER POETRY AWARD FOR 2017

*BOA wishes to acknowledge the generosity of the following
40 for 40 Major Gift Donors*

Lannan Foundation
Gouvernet Arts Fund
Angela Bonazinga & Catherine Lewis
Boo Poulin

BYE-BYE LAND

POEMS

CHRISTIAN BARTER

American Poets Continuum Series, No. 161

BOA Editions, Ltd. ❖ Rochester, NY ❖ 2017

First Edition
17 18 19 20 7 6 5 4 3 2 1

For information about permission to reuse any material from this book, please contact
The Permissions Company at www.permissionscompany.com or e-mail permdude@
gmail.com.

Publications by BOA Editions, Ltd.—a not-for-profit corporation
under section 501 (c) (3) of the United States Internal Revenue
Code—are made possible with funds from a variety of sourc-
es, including public funds from the Literature Program of the
National Endowment for the Arts; the New York State Council
on the Arts, a state agency; and the County of Monroe, NY.
Private funding sources include the Lannan Foundation for sup-
port of the Lannan Translations Selection Series; the Max and
Marian Farash Charitable Foundation; the Mary S. Mulligan
Charitable Trust; the Rochester AreaCommunity Foundation; the Steeple-Jack Fund; the
Ames-Amzalak Memorial Trust in memory of Henry Ames, Semon Amzalak, and Dan
Amzalak; and contributions from many individuals nationwide. See Colophon on page
112 for special individual acknowledgments.

ART WORKS.
arts.gov

State of the Arts

NYSCA

Cover Design: Sandy Knight
Cover Art: *Brooklyn Bridge* by Richard Margolis
Interior Design and Composition: Richard Foerster
BOA Logo: Mirko

Library of Congress Cataloging-in-Publication Data

Names: Barter, Christian, 1969– author.
Title: Bye-bye land / poems by Christian Barter.
Description: First Edition. | Rochester, NY : BOA Editions Ltd., 2017. |
    Series: American poets continuum series ; 161
Identifiers: LCCN 2016045566 (print) | LCCN 2016052989 (ebook) | ISBN
        9781942683353 | ISBN 9781942683360 (e-book)
Subjects: | BISAC: POETRY / American / General. | POLITICAL SCIENCE /
    Government / National. | POLITICAL SCIENCE / Political Ideologies /
    General.
Classification: LCC PS3602.A8386 A6 2017 (print) | LCC PS3602.A8386 (ebook)
| DDC 811/.6—dc23
LC record available at https://lccn.loc.gov/2016045566

BOA Editions, Ltd.
250 North Goodman Street, Suite 306
Rochester, NY 14607
www.boaeditions.org
A. Poulin, Jr., Founder (1938–1996)

Contents

(2008)

1

The Warm Land

A full moon hanging in the last part of the night,
a few crickets grinding it out a little longer,
their inner workings will not let them stop,
rhythm like a train climbing,
rhythm like a hammer,
a laundromat chorus of washing machines,
a mechanized loom threshing out the soft yarn

And the first cars in the distance humming
through New Jersey towards New York or Philly,
a pedal tone for some modal chant
that hasn't yet begun

And the moon, its plains and craters
bright and sharp, even from this distance,
especially from this distance,
silent partner
unchanged by all this commotion,
its silence unbroken by an early jet passing,

unchanged from the time of single cells, dividing,
to the creatures who can gaze at it now,
the fires always burning on their plains,
who have found the fire of the sun inside a rock.

Inside the house, the lights come on.
The man sits up, stares at the floor.
The woman covers her eyes with a blanket.
Did you sleep all right?
But there is only the sound of running water.

I dreamt again of the ships, the tall ships

Don't forget to take the garbage to the curb.
And call Visa about that overcharge, will you?
And we need to stop by the ShopRite—we're out of milk.
And don't forget the tank's about on empty.
Forget not yet the tried intent
Of such a truth as I have meant[1]

In the last part of the night
when the night is an ink spilled into water
and the things of this world have not yet made it back
from being skyline

◆

---

[1] Thomas Wyatt, "Forget Not Yet."

Ships, towers, domes, theaters, and temples,[2]
steel U-Store-Its, smokestacks, Golden Arches,
landfill mountains, gas-station islands
have not yet made it back from being skyline,
from being *one* line,
from being settled on the murky bottom
for divers' salvages, arriving alone,

the bus driver thrumming at his vinyl helm,
the new guy getting to the office early,
the halls one off the other, rooms
waiting for something, waiting
with an attitude you must catch them off guard to see—

Arriving alone, the fast-food manager,
the rows of plastic seats an empty chapel

White cereals in the whites of kitchens,
white bread, white noise of televisions

It's morning again in America.[3]

Fears of impending global financial crisis
The threat of terror
First of all, sir, the President has said
we are not going to engage in torture under any circumstances[4]
And the Philadelphia Phillies
have won the first of a possible seven games.

◆

---

[2] "Ships, towers, domes, theatres, and temples lie / Open unto the fields, and to the sky,"
William Wordsworth, "Composed upon Westminster Bridge, September 3, 1802."
[3] Ronald Reagan, campaign slogan of 1984.
[4] Alberto Gonzales, Attorney General confirmation hearing before Congress, January 6, 2005.

History is theirs and the people make it[5]

and tree to tree the starlings flit
and glide and fritter away the only hour
of the dawn—trees clenched,
trees heated and bent and doused in the cold water
of the day, the sky
a pale blue neither far nor near—

the sky that was over the Peloponnesians
sailing at Greece, the Etruscans
firing themselves on dishes to be smashed
by the Romans' thousand-year tantrum, the sky
they saw through the smoke of the ships at Veracruz,
the sky that absorbed the flag over Iwo Jima.

I guess everybody just trying to, ah,
pick up their game, you know?
And do everything we usually do,
just that much more harder and, you know,
that much more better.[6]

And what would the dogs do?

◈

---

[5] "History is ours and the people make it," Salvador Allende.
[6] from an interview with Eddie House, Boston Celtic, after a game in 2008.

The dog would hold on to my clothes and bite me.

Where did they bite you?

If they would let the dogs go they would definitely bite us.

When you got to Guantanamo what happened?

I could not see anything or hear anything,
and I was like that for about two weeks.[7]

And the trees that look too thick to cross,
the trees that flank the interstate,
the trees along a field's far edge,
their vines and branches clinging into clouds
the way the atom's forces draw
its spinnings into matter,

the engine noise and deadened barking
suspended in the trees themselves,
as though already memory:
of boys with basketballs and dogs
incensed by cars and muffled back doors
closing out of sight—the trees

that stand up at the city's edge
and dive up through the asphalt from their
secret tunnels, dug before the war—

trees that tower over every house
along a street where the talk runs on
like the fences, like the tar.

❖

[7] Adel Hamad, interview, with Amy Goodman, 31 May 2008. Transcript from humanrights. ucdavis.edu.

Hey, did you check traffic? Is there coffee?

My charger. The phone charger.

                              The briefcase. The keys.

No, the yellow one, honey, with the gold fringe.

                                        Where?

Did you talk to Kevin?

                    WHO'S coming over?

The dog, hon. Don't forget the dog.

                              We'll talk about it later.

No, Tessie, we're not wearing that today.
Because we're not. Go change it—okay?

          I love you. Love you! Love *you*. Love YOU.

Because we're not prostitutes, Tessie, that's why.

◈

I'm not saying I don't *like* it here.
Hold on, yah, I can hear you now.
It's a pretty town—it is—and I definitely
don't have to worry about getting attacked
on my way home from work or whatever.
But we're in bed at 9:30 every night!
It's not like I want to go out to the bars
and do the whole party-girl thing—*Woo-hoo!*
but I want to do *something* at night. It's like
Michael just decided: we're married now,
time to start acting like we're sixty.
I guess I just want something more out of my *existence*
on this *planet* than going to work and coming home
and watching *How I Met Your Mother*.
I know: I hated Philly—but I miss it, you know?
And Michael, he's a big help: *Let's go to Aruba!*
Like we're gonna come home to some different life.
Okay, he says, *you want to go back to Philly?*
You want to move to New York? How about Seattle?
And I'm like, sure, Michael, how *about* Seattle.
It's freakin' Seattle. There's a Space Needle.
Is anything really gonna be different?

❖

Let them come to New Jersey[8]

where everywhere the big sky flames
and trees spread out their solemn wings

And the roads are unbroken,
the roads that branch and branch,

the roads thrown down like a net on something wild
which stares back through it, roads like a thought
in front of what is real, a sentiment

that gives the mind an easy path—
the mind that keeps its eyes before its feet,

the mind, that would destroy the thing that is
to have the thing it can understand

❖

---

[8] "Let them come to Berlin." John F. Kennedy, 26 June 1963.

So you're asking me to answer a hypothetical.[9]

Jat Jamma?[10] I don't know, some grass hut name.
They ran right the fuck over this guy.
Can you imagine? Getting trampled to death
by fat chicks trying to save two bucks on a vacuum?
And this guy wasn't any midget, either.
They just stuck him out there, like, *Hold the door, pal.*
And what's he gonna do, say no?
GENTLEMEN GOOD MORNING
You see they laid off Jimmy-bird? I *told* him:
Jimmy, it's getting slow, you know?
Just show these guys you want the job, that's all.
SAME CREWS AS YESTERDAY ANY QUESTIONS
So I'm *done* with him. I'm done.
I mean, Jesus Christ, that job he did on Terlaine?
And he's like, *Oh, I got the carpal tunnel . . .*
AT YOUR LEISURE GENTLEMEN AT YOUR LEISURE
You coming, Tone? Guy was from Haiti.
Yah, he was like six-six, two-seventy.
A lot of fucking good that did him.

❖

---

[9] op. cit., Gonzales.
[10] Jdimytai Damour, a Walmart worker at Green Acres Mall in Valley Stream, New York, was trampled to death by shoppers the day after Thanksgiving in 2008.

Las sich nach New Jersey *Kommen*[11]

where everywhere the big sky flames,
where farm fields stretch their bodies under blankets
and streams push on through undergrowth,
on under highways, on around parking lots,

the bushes thrusting up through blanked backyards
like water blossoming from broken pipes

where, through that jungle, houses look like outposts,
thatched huts on islands that have never seen a ship.

So tractable, so peaceable are these people
that I swear to your Majesties
there is not in the world a better nation.[12]

With what *delight* could they have driven around,
if they could joy in aught; sweet interstate!
through hill and valley, rivers, woods, and plains—[13]

Oh, it was fucking gorgeous, I'm *tellin'* ya,
the sky so blue it looked like a *cartoon.*[14]

❖

---

[11] *Las sich nach Berlin Kommen* ("Let them come to Berlin"), op. cit., Kennedy.
[12] Columbus, in a letter to the King and Queen of Spain, about the Tainos (*Bury My Heart at Wounded Knee*, Dee Brown, pp. 1, 2)
[13] "With what delight could I have walked thee round, / If I could joy in aught, sweet interchange / Of hill and valley, rivers, woods, and plains." Milton, *Paradise Lost*, IX, 114–116.
[14] "The blue has never been so pure around the chimneys— / 'Almost like—a cartoon!' says the dental hygienist, / Grasping for a metaphor." Phillip Lopate, "Allende."

And these are the names of the men that shall stand with you:
of the tribe of Reuben: Elizur, the son of Shedeur;
of Simeon: Shelumiel, son of Zurishaddai;
of Judah: Nahshon the son of Amminadab.[15]

Of Harrison Ave, John Plinckett, brother of Corey.
Of Prospect Street, that guy who does duct work.
Professor Richardson, when he gets back from sabbatical.
Joey the Goose, originally from Brooklyn.
Allison Carter—yah, I know,
but she's got balls THIS BIG, you know what I'm sayin'?
And who's that guy there with the little mustache,
kind of a wack job, am I right?
But the guy can schedule a train like nobody's business.
I don't need to know about his personal life.

(They don't need to know about why the big sky flames
and trees spread out their solemn wings
while they stroll campuses and stand in break rooms,
talking into their hands, into the air.)

And I would say, I am just a normal worker,
and work, and get my salary.

Did you ever learn anyone's name?

They have no names. They have borrowed names. They have numbers.[16]

❖

---

[15] Numbers 1:5–7.
[16] op. cit., Adel Hamad interview.

They strolled the campuses. They stood in chapels.
They stood in chapels, under the huge stained glass.
They drifted in silent, powerful automobiles.
They lived like Tudors.

They lived in projects.
They strolled the grassless lawns.
They lived in trailers, surrounded by dogs.
They lived in Tudors.
They lived in the White House
surrounded by dogs and Secret Service.
They were surrounded by disembodied motors.

They worried about the economic climate,
the falling dollar, collateralized debt.
They divided their items at the supermarket:
what the food stamps covered, what they didn't.
They bought futures and shorts, blue chips and penny stocks.
"Spare change," they said outside the Starbucks.

They worried about melting glaciers.
They worried about getting shot in the stairwell.
They worried about eating carbs.
They worried about getting turned away at the hospital.

They sat on marble benches
watching water erupt from the angels' mouths.

They worked in automotive.
They worked the streets.
They were working in polyrhythms at the time.
Working the crowd. Working an angle.
Working every shift they could get.
Working the room. Working the land.
Working the theme of middle class ennui.
Working *it*. Working out.
Working in oils, working in clay.

Working in shit up to their knees.
Working on their marriages.
Working on their flaws.
Working together to bring peace to the Middle East.

One doesn't need to know their private intentions.
The work tells all.[17]

◆

---

[17] op. cit., Sontag.

And so we went there to the Warm Land.
We went to the terminus of a railroad and passed through
the land of the Osages and on to the land full of rocks,
and next morning we came to the land of the Kaws . . .
and we saw how the people of that land were . . .
and we thought those two tribes were not able to do much for
        themselves.[18]

I was there to *shop* but these people were, like,
ready to charge machine gun nests or something.
And then this chant broke out?
"Push the doors in! Push the doors in!"
And then the whole freakin' crowd just started to move,
and the only place to *go* was into the store—
I swear to God, at that moment—No, *skim* milk.
Do I sound like a Jersey bitch from hell, or what?
So anyway, we come *crashing* through the glass—
I didn't even see the guy, I'm telling you,
it was like a horror movie—just grunting and breathing
and God knows *who*, like, thrusting into me.
And I see the guy lying there and everything—
I mean, what was I supposed to *do*?
And now everybody's like, "You *bought* somethin'?"
Like I killed the guy by buying a freakin' camera.

❖

---

[18] White Eagle, on being shown his new reservation, from *Bury My Heart at Wounded Knee*,
Dee Brown, p. 409.

In the last part of the last part of the night
which is morning, which is day, which is filled with light,

a light that is like a silence behind the noise,
a light that becomes what it touches,
a light that is like a love so deep
you don't even know it's there—

This' hard work, boss, wait' for The Word.[19]

Light squandering itself on the hoods of cars,
light pooling in leaves and lying flat on asphalt
and boring down into the tiny caves of the grass,

a light that is everywhere and therefore nowhere,
a light that is asking you to answer a hypothetical,
a light that has lit up Lawrenceville like a *lamp*.

❖

---

[19] John Berryman, Dream Song 10.

This' hard work, boss, gettin' rid of all these trees.
They big and they solid and they been here awhile.
And these birds, boss—shit, you try catching
just one of 'em. We gonna have to pave
the whole damn place if you want *them* to go away.
And I'm gonna need more labor, boss—
these slave ships, they a drop in the bucket, boss;
I need Chinese, Irish, Japanese,
and whatever you can get me from Mexico, boss.
We got diggin' to do, and cuttin' stuff down,
and blowin' stuff up, and settin' stuff on fire.
And what do you want to do about all this sky?
It's bigger than it looks, and for all these chimneys,
the blue keeps coming back. I reckon
we gonna have to give every man and woman
their own, personal way of makin' smoke.
Just wake 'em up early and get 'em movin,'
the way you move a herd on a cold night
so as they don't freeze to death—and not let 'em rest, boss.
I know I'm askin' for a lot, boss.
But you want the job done right.

◆

And so we went there to the Warm Land.
We passed by the projects and the Quickie Marts
and we wound through the looping miles of suburbs
where every house and hairdo looked the same,
and I saw how the people of that land were
and I thought they were not able to do much for themselves—
they were forced to leave their homes all day
and their children played behind metal fences.
And I saw how the trees were
and how the ground was covered with black tar.
And I saw the looks on the faces of these people.

We passed down into the hollows of a train station,
into a cave where the trains jarred the floor
and I saw how these people were,
how close they were pressed together,
how afraid they were to smile at each other,
for the killers walked among them
and those who would sell the tally machines
to count up the souls in the camps
and those who waited for the others to get sick
so they could come for their houses walked among them
and those whom anger had touched too deeply,
who had crouched deep into the foxholes of themselves
or crawled deep into the wooden horse of sadness
and those who would watch you gang-raped from the window
and those who saw the demon everywhere
longing only for one chance at its throat—

◈

Hon, we should get that hibachi back to Oliver.
Does it still have coals in the bottom, sweetheart?
God it's gorgeous out, isn't it?
I have never seen so many birds!
Look at that fat little guy on the dead branch.
And the sheep? We really lucked out with this spot.
Remember the place we looked at downtown?
Above the bar? Can you imagine?
Oh, damn, it's Karen. Hello?

Out past the field, out past the trees
out past the dark that fills their passageways—

always disappearing as I approach

That's way too much work for one person, Karen.
They're not going to give you any help with this thing?

out past the last blue ceiling bending down
behind the woods to touch the ground again

when I come out from the trees to find them:

the tall ships in the harbor, floating, waiting,
with not a soul on board,
their decks as worn and smooth as driftwood

You have to sit down with your boss, Karen.
And if he won't listen, you have to go to *his* boss.

❖

2

The Meaning of Being Numerous

> "And Thee, across the harbor, silver-paced
> As though the sun took step of thee, yet left
> Some motion ever unspent in thy stride,—
> Implicitly thy freedom staying thee!"
> —Hart Crane, *The Bridge*

> "One must have deeper motives and judge everything accordingly,
> but go on talking like an ordinary person."
> —Pascal, *Pensées*

Brilliant city! a crystal blooming
in a cave floor, toylike, tiny, near
and distant—clarified by distance
to something clean enough to touch,
like a battle cleansed by history—

Pristine city—looking back
from the Verrazano, or over from a dock
in Red Hook, Manhattan
like a constellation
unable to break free of the earth—

A cluster of pinholes in a cell-black sky
that lets light through from the fire blazing beyond it—

Unable to break free of the earth,
taking the turns they have always taken,
they cross Fifth Avenue, the Brooklyn Bridge,
more absolute than ever,[20]
Manhattan like a consolation
for the caged dark of these crossings,
for the turns they have taken and cannot take back.

And they go on talking like ordinary people

---

[20] "and this truth, now proved, / That made me exile in her streets, stood me / More absolute than ever." Hart Crane, *The Bridge*.

In the halls of high buildings, in the backs of cabs,
in the giant foyer of the Museum of Natural History,
in the Lysol-armored seats of cineplexes,
at The Statue with its bronzed broken shackles,
standing watch for the next hull-load,
and under those little tarp-things where the doormen
stand watch against an army of the homeless,
In the hush of the MoMA, broken only
by the buzzing of incoming texts

wherever the Just exchange their messages[21]

Manhattan like a compensation,
trinkets for what used to be the night.

◈

---

[21] W. H. Auden, "September, 1, 1939."

Oh yah, they walkin' around like Professor Dumbledore
with their hands behind their backs, face all scrunched up
like somebody just pass gas and they the one
been put in charge of the Central Committee
on Finding Out Whose Butt It Was.
Oh, they got all this stuff here figured *right* out.
It's all "this period" and "that period,"
and the "use" of this, and how "bold" somebody was.
"That was *bold*," they say, going after the chin.
"That was a *bold use* of color." "What a *bold line!*"
I tell you what—if drawin' on some paper? Is *bold?*
Bold. You'd think with all these geniuses
this wouldn't be a such a fucked-up place to live.
I'd like to round up all these geniuses
and say, Now how come all this killing going on?
And how come all these kids come home from school
and they don't know nothing? They can't *add*,
they can't read a *book.* And why is it *the case*
my mama work thirty years up in that home
changing old men's diapers and if *she* go
up to see the doctor, they all
Ma'am, what kinda insurance has you got?
Now if you could all just pull yourselves away
from these here soup cans—Oh, yah! Soup cans is *big.*
And they *bold*, too, if everybody right.
You got a stain. Right there. No, let me get it.
These white uniforms—you can't even
get within a hundred feet of food, hon.

What about a case here, an American citizen,
in the United States?[22]

❖

---

[22] Senator Biden questioning Alberto Gonzales about U.S. use of torture, on January 6, 2005.

The elephant in the room is *brontosaurus*,
his neck stacked high
to the inbred royalty of his tiny head,
his ribcage showing through to more of themselves:

they who walk among the bones for hours—

Protoceratops, allosaurus,
stripped down by dust to just their armor,
the brutal shields and horns and teeth
the only things left to tell us what they were,
like a box of old letters,
or a chimney standing in the ashes of a house

Your Reverence writes me that you would like to know
whether the Negroes who are sent to your parts
have been legally captured [23]

What killed them, Mommy?

An asteroid.

What's that?

To this I reply that I think Your Reverence
should have no scruples on this point, because

What's that. Okay.
At night, you know how you can see the stars?
The earth is like a—like a big balloon.

---

[23] Letter from Brother Luis Brandaon, March 12, 1610, continuing: "To this I reply that I think your Reverence should have no scruples on this point, because this is a matter which has been questioned by the Board of Conscience in Lisbon, and all its members are learned and conscientious men. Nor did the bishops who were in São Thomé, Cape Verde, and here in Loando—all learned and virtuous men—find fault with it."

It floats around. And we're stuck to the balloon.
Or, like a boat—in the biggest ocean ever—

because, because, because, because, because

◈

And the city breathed.
It heaved and sighed.
The groans of lifting heavy stones.
It squeaked and clanged.
Whole villages slid by on rails.
The frantic boredom of car horns.
The war-whoop of sirens coming down from far-off hills.
All of it like a silence.
Like a stutter.
A disturbed man shouting the same words over and over.
What do you think it means, doc?
Well, I don't know.
Sometimes these things don't really MEAN anything.
Metal on metal, fumes exploding in chambers.
Air brakes crashing like waves
sent in by a storm that hit Haiti days ago.

❖

Dude, you made it. Sweet. You need a beer.
This is Mauriana. Whitney. Bela.
And *this* is the art salon. Check it out.
Oh, man, have you even *heard* the 10,000 Maniacs
in years? I love it. Turn it up!
It's like they're good all over again.
This guy does installation pieces.
You sticking around for the reading?
This one's a faucet—pouring out of the *water*.
Right? And this thing here—
well, I guess I don't know *what* this is.
Some kind of po-mo parakeet. I love it.
Dude, what the fuck? You need another tall boy?
Look at this thing. It's a grouchy Buddha
squatting down a teeter-totter.
"Pudgy Wins." I love it. What do you think?

I dreamt last night I was lying on my back
and a man was pointing out the constellations,
and as he spoke, the stars lit up in patterns:

Dude, check *this* out: his afro's made of pennies

a chain of light, a double helix,
two clusters of tiny stars like twin clouds.
They were so real, so bright that you could see
their very distances. And then I felt
the distance, I felt how far they were—

❖

It is dark along the streets, bright high in the buildings,
bright past the buildings where Manhattan stands
in a robe of light. Its light is like an argument,
an argument it makes with each man looking,
an argument that will not be talked down.

The dark is local. The light takes over
the farther one looks away. The light is public.
It insists on life. On hope.
The light would never pull the plug.
The light cares nothing for misery.
The light only acknowledges positive feedback.
The light is a conversation at a party
where every private fear is polluted with confidence.

◈

It's good to be with you, Dana. What's happened so far
is they've charged Plaxico with a class C felony[24]
for having the gun illegally, which carries
a minimum sentence of three and a half years.
The fact that it went off in his pocket may lengthen that.
Hey, look, I know it's rough out there, Dana,
especially in some of the neighborhoods these players come from,
but he's let a lot of people down here—
people who really love football, Dana,
who love to see bone-crunching hits, Dana,
and huge men knocking each other unconscious,
banging heads on the gridiron, Dana.
They just can't understand this kind of behavior.

Oh, Dana, Dana, Dana, Dana, Dana—

◈

---

[24] On November 28, 2008, Plaxico Burress suffered an accidental self-inflicted gunshot
wound to the right thigh; two days later, he turned himself in to police to face charges of
criminal possession of a handgun.

I mean, here's Frickie, with his hand out like *this*—
like a special-needs kid at the petting zoo,
trying to touch that girl's bald head—
And I'm, like, *No, this is not happening.*
LADIES AND GENTLEMEN WE HAVE A RED LIGHT
AND WE SHOULD BE MOVING SHORTLY
And she wheels around like the fucking *Exorcist*,
and says, "I have cancer, you piece of shit,"
and Frickie's like, "Whoa," and I'm like, *FUCK,*
Frickie did not just step in it that deep.
But of course he did! Frickie *always* steps in it that deep!
And what do you think he says? *Sorry?*

And we walked through the shanty town of streets
tacked up at the feet of the towers of Manhattan.
The night came down on us and we walked fast,
the barely chained dogs of the traffic sniffing near us,
the barely chained dogs on each face passing
in the miles of night, and we tried to forget our boredom,
and we threw our ships on the first sea that washed up to us,
and we threw our words at whatever gods
were in the flight paths over us,
like children heaving rocks at the moon,
like grown men heaving rockets at the moon—

◈

Your Reverence, surely, knows the score.
Your Reverence has read Machiavelli and Darwin.
Your Reverence has observed the praying mantis,
has witnessed the ocean receding under
the moon's inexorable draw, has seen
the virus under the microscope.
Your Reverence has seen what people do to each other
in off-shore prisons and trailer park bedrooms.

We are neither God nor Christ, Your Reverence.
We only insult them by such comparisons,
be it by word or deed.
We live as man in the world God made for us,
where survival of one means death of another,
where freedom of one means servitude of another,
where *the Lord doth put a difference
between the Egyptians and Israel—*[25]

where if one soul is to enter the blessed kingdom
another must writhe in the flames of hell
for all eternity, with no hope of reprieve.

Perhaps, Your Reverence, you and I
would not have chosen it this way. But choice,
as long as the Almighty reigns in heaven,
will never be man's lot. *Your faithful servant*

◈

---

[25] Exodus, 11:7.

Did they just walk right over him?[26]
Do you think they saw him?
Did they run away when the police came?
Where's Haiti?
Where's Walmart?
What does Walmart look like?
Does anybody still go there?
What's a temp worker?

Tell me the story of The Gingerbread House.
Tell me the story of the dinosaurs.

How far is the Walmart from our house?

Ms. Kasrel says, if you go far enough
you end up where you started.

But Calvin says you end up out in space.

◆

---

[26] cf. "Bad Time Stories," Judith Warner, *The New York Times*, 4 December 2008. The op-ed article is about a mother being questioned by her seven-year-old daughter about Jdimytai Damour, trampled to death by shoppers on November 28, 2008, at a Walmart in Valley Stream, New York.

Thank you. Thank you for having me up here.
It's really something, all of this. I mean—
there's a theory going around that art is useless,
but I think I need only turn your attention
to this faucet here, to explode that myth.
I mean, anybody thirsty? For a *faucet*?
Oh man, I love this stuff, I really do.

> The Emancipation Proclamation
> Feels as good as masturbation.

Thank you. Thank you so much. I just wrote that one.
I'm very into rhyme, you know?
Actually, fuck rhyme. I just changed my mind.
I'm so glad you guys were here for this.
Call me Constantine, right? I mean, what was up
with *that* dude? "Give me the God who helps me
slaughter the most people!" I'm sorry, folks,
what a boring topic. But battleground conversions—
I think all poems are battleground conversions.
You're sitting there, scared off your ass, yet hoping
for everything. Take these lines by Oppen:

> Obsessed, bewildered
>
> By the shipwreck
> Of the singular
>
> We have chosen the meaning
> Of being numerous.[27]

Actually, I have no idea what that poem means.
Bad example. But don't you just *feel*
that this guy is about to go careening down the hill
with his broadsword waving, shouting,

---

[27] Of Being Numerous, 7, *George Oppen*.

"We have chosen the meaning of being numerous!"
I don't have any idea what Oppen looked like,
but I tend to picture him as about six-eight,
two-sixty, ripped muscle—no, wait, that's Brandon Jacobs;
his poetry is running the *football*, man. "Inquiry":

> Where were you when the towers fell?
> When Kennedy was shot?
> The first one?
> By that lone gun-mun?
> Wink, wink?
> No, seriously, though, where were you?

You see what I did there? Showed a poem
trying to exist in the real world, which it can't—
don't ask me why—the helmsman put it down
as *law*: [28] poetry makes nothing *happen* . . . dudes. [29]
I know, I know—I'm starting to rant.
I might as well be waving my broadsword around—
"We have chosen the meaning of being numerous!"
Okay, okay. "Poem Beginning with a Line
by Oppen and Ending with a Line by e. e. cummings":

> Obsessed, bewildered
> By the shipwreck of the singular,
> He spoke—and drank rapidly a glass of water. [30]

See how everything, in spite of your best efforts
to fragment things, just wants to gel together?
Meaning is like a—like a fucking weed.
That's why you don't have to be smart to be a poet.
It's as easy as putting pennies on an afro.

---

[28] "[T]he helmsman lays it down as law / that we must suffer, suffer into truth." Aeschylus, *Agamemnon*.
[29] "For poetry makes nothing happen," W. H. Auden, "In Memory of W. B. Yeats."
[30] E. E. Cummings, "next to of course god america i."

I love that sculpture, though—seriously.
Though I just had the sudden urge to change that last line to:
"He spoke—and drank rapidly a glass of *faucets*."
No, sorry, that's awful. A glass of *faucets*?
That's the problem with conversions: you get *hooked*.
It's such a *rush*, changing what you believe:
There's no such thing as climate change. Holy crap!
Grab that floating piece of garbage, dude!
If I could, I'd change what I believe
every second of the day. No, I'm sorry, that's stupid.
I love the sculptures, though, man, I really do.
They have chosen the meaning of being numerous.
Don't ever change! Actually, I mean,
if you see a pattern in your work, smash it.[31]
By the way, do you see what hell's like?
People who won't shut up. Am I right?
You read *The Inferno* lately?
"Blabbety blat, I fucked Armando"—
It's like a bunch of people on cell phones,
eternal damnation. And do you still think
it's so imperative to *fornicate*,
and fill your bodies with *substances*?
Is it really worth those moments of ecstasy—
those moments you see eye to eye with God—
those moments you think you might be a god yourself?
A forgotten god—wandering in the wreckage—

◈

---

[31] Pablo Picasso.

3

And All the Lives to Be

"In Hamdi, the Court said the United States could detain an American citizen, here in this country, for the duration of the hostilities, without filing charges."
—Alberto Gonzales

"O God, I could be bounded in a nutshell and count myself as king of infinite space, were it not that I have bad dreams."
—Hamlet

The cars are stopped on the interstate four lanes wide
a glorious autumn Saturday, pointed away,
trying to get to the lakes and hills and trees,
ten or fifteen miles of stopped cars.

There is not enough room for them anymore.
There is not enough room for them or for their smoke.

Stopped cars jammed in the neck of the timer,
stopped cars stacked like a steeple into distance—

An army at the tall gates, waiting, waiting
for the signal—a flare, a gunshot,
or, *What? Do you sons of bitches want to live forever?*[32]

Ten thousand hunched in shelters at cell phones and radios
as though something very bad had happened.

We'll go over the actual phone call later
to the nine-one-one operator—
through a translator, of course;
it's not like these people speak English—

---

[32] Marine Sergeant Dan Daly, at the Battle of Belleau Woods in World War I.

They would like to go to the Poconos.
They would like to step out of their cars and go walking
beneath the enormous sky[33]

Stopped as though every citizen of this country
as well as the members of Congress
were considering the matter carefully—[34]

Why don't you just try the other lane, sweetie?

Because I can't get into it, sweetie.

I'll signal someone to let us in.

They're not going anywhere either.

He's letting us in, hon—look—he's letting us in.

Let's just sit here and wait, okay?

But he's LETTING US IN.

I'm asking you to believe.
Not just in my ability to bring about real change in Washington.[35]

◆

---

[33] "I would like to step out of my heart / and go walking beneath the enormous sky." Rainer Maria Rilke, "Lament."
[34] "I believe we should go to the moon. But I think every citizen of this country as well as the Members of Congress should consider the matter carefully." John F. Kennedy, May 25, 1961.
[35] Barack Obama, campaign slogan, 2008.

Can you find out what his emergency is, please?

I'm at the emergency room.
My girlfriend is dying, and the nurses don't want to help her.

What does he mean, she's dying? What's wrong with her?

She's vomiting blood.
They're not doing anything, just watching her.

Okay. He needs to contact a nurse
and let them know she's vomiting blood.[36]

◈

---

[36] From the text of a 911 call made from a hospital by the boyfriend of Edith Rodriguez, who died of a perforated bowel after lying for forty-five minutes on the floor of an emergency room on May 9, 2007. The boyfriend was requesting that an ambulance be sent to the hospital. (lines 1–8)

For the duration of the hostilities[37]
Until there's an end to the war
Until high-pilèd books in charact'ry
Hold like rich garners the full-ripened grain[38]
As long as there is evil in the world, my friends
Until we can say for certain American lives
And the vessels of the potter are broken to shivers[39]
And the fight is over and we have laid down our backpack nukes
And beat our swords into microchips
And all the lives we ever lived,
And all the lives to be[40]
And the bad dogs barking from the impoundment lot
And the dealers barking from the bad blocks
And the unborn in the womb and their unborn

◈

---

[37] op. cit., Gonzales, Senate testimony, 2005.
[38] John Keats, "When I Have Fears That I May Cease to Be."
[39] "As the vessels of a potter shall they be broken to shivers." Revelation, 2:27.
[40] Charles Elton, "Luriana, Lurilee."

They'll be stopped in a minute, too, just like us.

I guess we'll just sit here and wait then, is that what you want?

I would like to step out of my heart and go walking.

And in this stained-glass ceiling blue,
the stopped cars climb the next crest out of sight,
becoming something as the distance takes them,
connecting to become a gleaming river
that cuts its way through trees that fuse to cliffs.

How everything just wants to gel together!
How, given distance, even cars clogged up
on the interstate four lanes wide *become*—

And the sky, its paneless window washed with light—
what do they want to do about all this sky,

sitting alone in submarines, in space shuttles,

arriving alone at the party with a dish
and a mouthful of fragments, a mouth full of dust?

❖

The *good* news is, I think it's finally over.
He's got that look. I know that look.
I think he's finally going to cave.
Hey, he'll still be the richest taco maker in Jersey.
Do I sound harsh? It's been a long day.
Listen, hon, did you feed Amanda?
Yah, I left a bottle in the fridge.
One's old, so look at the dates. Uh huh. She DID?
You're kidding. Well, I hope you got it on video.
Can you believe how fast this is all going?
HEY, JERK-WAD, LET'S MOVE IT ALONG, SHALL WE?
How'd *your* day go? Did you call José?
Well, we have to do *something* about the driveway, hon.
It's only going to get worse. No, no, I'm fine.
These cases are always just tough.
I mean, they really try to get to you:
Here's Martino riding his bike,
and here's Martino with a big, fat little-boy smile—
on the front porch, by the way, of that firetrap.
BUDDY WILL YOU PLEASE GET YOUR THUMB OUT OF
       YOUR ASS.
Are you going to tell me it's safer in Tijuana?
I'm sorry. It's been a long day. It's just work, right?
Call José about the driveway, though.
Another big rain and we'll lose the whole thing.

❖

What does he mean she's dying?
What's wrong with her?
Is she bursting into flames?
Is she crumbling to dust?
Did she turn into a shadow on the sidewalk?
A pillar of salt? Has she turned to a pillar of salt, sir?

I'm afraid there isn't a whole lot we can do
until we know what's going on here.

Only then will this nation move forward
with the full speed of freedom.[41]

Just WHAT was the expectation there?
Transportation to another Hospital?
The article says NOTHING
about HOW the bowels became perforated . . .
Drugs? Gang Violence? Abuse?
How likely is this that it just spontaneously occurred
and they walked calmly to the hospital?
THIS IS HEALTHCARE UNDER HILLARY CLINTON!!
It is likely healthcare under AMNESTY TOO
because in short order THEY will be the Majority
and then this whole glass house of cards
is going Click Click BOOM to Bye-bye Land.[42]

When I was young I walked all over this country,
east and west, and saw no other people.[43]

◈

----

[41] "[T]his nation will move forward, with the full speed of freedom, in the exciting adventure of space." John F. Kennedy, May 25, 1961.

[42] This stanza is quoted from a blog post in response to the Rodriguez death.

[43] "When I was young I walked all over this country, east and west, and saw no other people than the Apaches." Cochise of the Chiricahua Apaches.

And the day has dusted the last far corners clean
and the guardrails, shoulders, signs, and roadside grass-strips
are dusted clean, are pulled out clean
from the fire, trees raked clean
between their smallest crevices, a swamp

raked clean beside the road, its silvered driftwood
bright as metal, stood up in the mud
that is burning inward from its edge
with thick grass and is cut through by a stream

the way a life is cut through by its passion—

Ah, don't—don't make this a giant deal—

Another world along the interstate,
this swamp that ekes its way back to sky

I'm just stuck in traffic, that's all this is.
It hasn't got nothing to do with her

this room where the dead are stood up with the living,
talking of the old life as though nothing had changed.

❖

I'm coming, aren't I? I just don't want to see her.
And I don't want to see *him* either, you know what I'm saying?
And I'm not going downstairs to look at his Penn State
        Bobbleheads—

Hey, anybody give that guy that news yet
that we graduated like ten fucking years ago?

And in dreams, when I have reached the highest story
and stepped out into the room of glass—

when I have left the town behind me
and am driving towards the tall cliffs, always
the tall cliffs standing at the ends of things—

when I have come through the darkness into the hall,
the great hall with its forest of stone pillars,

she meets me there, she is with me there,
unlosable and unobtainable,

she fucking stands there fucking looking at me—

❖

Were it not that they have bad dreams

they could be bounded in a roll cage,
bounded in a role,
bounded in a variable-rate mortgage,

bounded in a cubicle, bounded in a prefab,
bounded by a blue sky—

Tristi fummo
ne l'aere dolce che dal sol s'allegra—[44]

bounded by a Bluetooth,
bounded to a ship mast,
bounded in cities cast of solid iron—[45]

Honey, I'll signal someone to let us in

O God they could be bounded to a PLANET
and count themselves as kings of infinite space—

❖

---

[44] "Once we were grim and sullen in the sweet air above." Dante, *Inferno*, Canto 7, lines 121–22, transl. Robert Pinsky.
[45] "The walls of that bleak city, which seemed cast / Of solid iron," ibid., Canto 8, lines 77–78.

Now, down here in Georgia we call that The Nuclear Option.

> Well, that's my point: *the nuclear option.*
> Everybody knows you can't launch those things.
> The players know it, the owners know it.
> Look, I was *around* for the Cuban Missile Crisis:
> "We're gonna have nuclear war! We're all gonna die!"
> And what happened? Nothing. Zitto. Zilch.

Zitto?

> But we came close, Dick.

> Close! I don't want to hear about close!
> Either you push the button or you don't!

Boomer?

> Well, I'm gonna have to ride the fence a little.
> I mean, The Goose is right that someone could "launch"—

Ride the fence? You're gonna "ride the fence"?

> Sit on the fence, whatever. Look, my point—

Boom, that was eloquent. Really. And you smell good, too.
You people at home, you can't smell this guy,
but I'm sitting next to him, and let me tell you—
Coach Dick, you smell that? Lilac? Persimmon?
Everybody lean in here, help me out;
it's like a—like a *mushroom cloud* of fragrance—

Come out and climb the garden path,
Luriana, Lurilee.[46]

◆

---

[46] op. cit., Elton.

The China rose is all abloom
And buzzing with the yellow bee[47]

Oh, it doesn't look good. It doesn't look good.
Oh, Jesus, this is not good. It's like
somebody just hit a beer can with a hammer.
OKAY, OKAY. JESUS, BUDDY.
Oh, shit—there's some guy just standing there.
And there's like all these tracks going off the road.
He's just standing all by himself at the edge of the road.

What does he mean, they're dying? What's wrong with them?
What does he mean the glaciers are melting?
What does he mean the oceans are full of mercury?
What does he mean their system of government
can no longer pass any meaningful laws?
What laws?
What does he mean they've killed half a million Iraqis?
Who?

Wow, that was rough. Sorry to be such a downer.
And now—big surprise—I have to pee.
I think I've had to pee for like an hour.
JUST PASS ME ALREADY. Has anybody showed up yet?
Hey—am I going to be the only single girl?
It's fine, I just—God, what is *wrong* with me?
I just keep meeting these *losers*.
YAH THAT'S IT BUDDY THERE YOU GO.

At least we're moving again. God, that *guy*.
It's like, great, I'm gonna have nightmares now, you know?

❖

---

[47] op. cit., Elton.

4

Secret Evidence

"The world is very different now. For man holds in his mortal hands
the power to abolish all forms of human poverty and all forms of
human life."
                              —John F. Kennedy

"They also serve who only stand and wait."
                              —John Milton

They are blowing the leaves from the grass at Princeton
boringly loud, an October morning,
while under the trees unleaving
unflappable statues balance declarations
on the backs of eagles and point their blank-eyed
horses home, where the paths crisscross

from church and lecture hall—the bags and backpacks,
the books and papers, phones out in front
(the world is very different now),
one Asian woman passing with a painting—

the coffees and teas, the chapels climbing
by steep roof lines the stairs to an ancient heaven,
the muscley columns pushing up marble,
the well-hoed gardens pushing up viburnum,
the Gothic library recalling a time
before movable type, one woman's curve
in a granite Lipchitz, a group of girls

laughing at how people miss
the most obvious truths, *I mean, right?*
a young lord on a skateboard
with his mind on his manor and his manor on his mind[48]

---

[48] "Rollin down the street, smokin indo, sippin on gin and juice / Laid back [with my mind
on my money and my money on my mind]" Snoop Dogg, "Gin and Juice."

and always somewhere just out of sight
that leaf-blower's groan of lifting a heavy stone,
and someone, or something, pulling the rope of the bells
come back to tell them all, *I shall tell you all*—[49]

◈

[49] "To say: 'I am Lazarus, come from the dead, / Come back to tell you all, I shall tell you all'—" T. S. Eliot, "The Love Song of J. Alfred Prufrock."

It all makes you feel very civilized, doesn't it?
All these medieval buildings, all this stone—
It's that old conservative impulse, I suppose.
It's very beautiful. Of course, when I was at Yale
we looked down our noses at all of this—
we thought of Princeton as the kind of place
you went if you were into the *status quo.*
The question of our time: the *status quo.*
We thought it *mattered* if we agreed with Nixon.
Mostly, of course, we argued with our fathers.
But what do *you* think? You're the one who's here.
It seems like kids now more or less accept things—
Iraq, Afghanistan, our criminal healthcare.
Ah, I don't know, maybe these kids are right.
We stood out here and waved our signs and still
we've got what we've got. You really can't blame them
for thinking our protests were just as much
bullshit as Bush is—and, perhaps, Obama.
But Jesus Christ, at least we stood for *something.*
What do you think? What's on that mind of yours?
Do thoughts grow like feathers, the dead end of life?[50]
I'll be thinking of you while I'm grinding it out
in Brooklyn, reading my students' vampire stories.
What *is* it with vampires these days, anyway?

◆

---

[50] W. H. Auden, "What's in Your Mind, My Dove, My Coney?"

They are passing with paintings, passing with upright basses.
They will never compromise their principles or standards.
They will never give away their freedom.
And they will never stop searching for a genuine peace.[51]

Remember how it was, to be a YOUNG nigga?[52]
toting Shakespeare or Einstein or Hobbes or Marx
or a sheaf of one's own—this paper is on
the Weimar Republic, and this one here
is a reimagining of the prophetess Cassandra
as a woman in love with the beauty of her visions

And these are their poems, and these are their novellas

and I wept much, because no man was found worthy
to open and to read the book.[53]

❖

---

[51] "[W]e will never compromise our principles and standards. We will never give away our freedom. [. . .] And we will never stop searching for a genuine peace. But we can assure none of these things America stands for through the so-called nuclear freeze solutions proposed by some." Ronald Reagan, "Evil Empire" speech, March 8, 1983.
[52] 2Pac, "Young Niggaz."
[53] Revelation, 5:4.

The huge cathedral windows dwarfed them
and let in shafts of light that lit their faces,
that washed their faces almost featureless.

In this time of transition, where we still find ourselves—[54]
He had been from Tehran to Lebanon,
and certainly Iraq was part of that,
having just succeeded in another election.
And as conditions continue to improve—[55]

The professors looked on solemnly.
One troubled one near the back kept turning
his pen in his hand like he was spindling
an invisible thread, rolling it up perfectly—

and clearly they also needed to move economically—

Now, there are a lot of ways to serve out there—
here in our own country, or you can serve globally.[56]

Then he took questions: *Sir, we're honored.*
Sir, we're proud. We're grateful, sir,
for your service to our country, sir,

in the shafts of light that stained the walls' stones
white as open sky.

❖

---

[54] Admiral Michael Mullen, Chairman of the Joint Chiefs, in an address at Princeton University on February 5, 2009.
[55] ibid.
[56] ibid.

It's not that there isn't wonderful work going on here.
Mind if we sit down and catch our breath?
Do you know Paul Krugman? Nice spot, huh?
Ah. "Martin Weitzman, a Harvard economist
offers some sobering numbers.
He argues that, overall, they suggest about
a five percent chance that world temperatures
will eventually rise by more than ten degrees"—[57]
Well, you know all about this stuff.
The crazy thing is, we *all* know all about it.
That's what's so incredible. All but the dumbest.
Do you know that sixty percent of young Americans
can't find Iraq on a map?[58] And each gets a vote.
Not that voting really changes anything.
Nothing really changes things anymore, does it?
We all keep talking about reducing emissions
and every year our emissions go up.
It's as though somewhere along the line
we got talking confused with actually doing something—

. . . making of love or counting of money,
Or raid on the jewels, the plans of a thief [59]

❖

---

[57] Paraphrased from Paul Krugman, "Can This Planet Be Saved?" *The New York Times*, August 1, 2008.
[58] Roper poll for *National Geographic*, 18 to 24-year-olds, 2006.
[59] op. cit., Auden.

They walked as they walked in the capitals of empires,
as though the day, at the least, belonged to them,
through the sculptures and statues, fountains and gardens,
a sparse and regal forest through it all
through which these few could pass whenever they wished
just as they were, in jeans and sneakers

and they don't ask why, they just ask what their mission is
because that's what they pledged to do when they raised their right
> *hand*[60]

toting Shakespeare or Einstein or Hobbes or Marx
or a sheaf of one's own, the hefty paper
slung about the neck in weighty silence

There was a ship[61]

This paper is on the fall of the Roman Empire,
and this one is on the trial of Socrates—

Galileo, Bonhoeffer, Jeanne d'Arc, Dred Scott—

Amadou Diallo, Rodney King, Omar Ahmed Khadr

❖

---

[60] op. cit., Mullen.
[61] "'There was a ship,' quoth he." Samuel Taylor Coleridge, "The Rime of the Ancient Mariner."

I've been doing a lot of thinking

The techno music at the café pounds its ramrod
on a giant gate, its three-note bass line
sunken and pleading, pleading with the stardust of the groin

I know I said that and that's how I felt at the time

And the standing up, the fumbling of the shawl,
the ironed and blow-dried, sheened black hair

But since then I've been doing a lot of thinking

A noise from her throat that is not unlike
a door closing slowly on old hinges,
the slipping hug falling off her like a dust—

as the others go on chatting, go on typing,
at the Small World Café, their white cells sweeping
up microtumors and the line keeps moving
keeps staying just as is

I set sail for Italy—all against my will[62]

Rhythm like a train climbing, rhythm like a hammer

Long before I was twenty-one men called me, "Mr. Rockefeller"[63]

the techno pounding from that deep recess
where sex and war and Jesus meet
our deep eternal theme[64]

---

[62] Virgil, *Aeneid*, Book 4, lines 451–52, transl. by Robert Fagles.
[63] John D. Rockefeller, quoted in *Titan*, Ron Chernow, p. 65.
[64] John Keats, "On Sitting Down to Read *King Lear* Once Again."

Whenever the darkness shrouds the earth,
whenever the stars go flaming up the sky,
my father's anxious voice warns me in dreams:[65]

Remember to wrap that weasel, Bryce—
you're not just having sex with her
you're having sex with everyone she's had sex with.

Oh, the world *is* very different now.

◈

---

[65] Cf., Virgil, op. cit., lines 438-41.

where paths crisscross from church and lecture hall
and a chapel climbs by steep roof lines the sky

for man holds in his mortal hands the power
to turn the pages of *The New Yorker*,
to work the Wii controller,
to check the ballot for A or B
and occasionally a spoiler—

and certainly Iraq is a part of that—

to take I-95 or 206
or drive out through the farms on Carter Road
and look at the sheep standing stock in their hunched files
beneath the enormous sky—

the sky that was the sky to the Lenape,
the sky that drafted the smoke of Troy.

❖

The dreams kept me busy from a young age.
They were so much more real
than what was supposed to be real:
the normal things of life—the gossip, sports,
small talk, the endless speeches of Hector
and Paris and my poor old father, who thought
that they were the only virtue left on earth
the way they went on about the infidels
gathering outside as though they hadn't brought
that shit upon themselves. But in the dreams—
the pure brilliance of the sky, the clear pools,
the sheer cliffs towering at the edge of sight—
if there are gods this is how they must see things.
They were, of course, the things of life, and yet
transformed, through rapture—or distress—
Maybe that's why no one ever believed me:
I always spoke as one entranced by death.
Oh, the beautiful horse I saw! It stood
at dawn on a silent, sleeping field, the soldiers
gone from the shores, the eye-blue ocean reaching
beyond the horizon, the silence of the fields—
So tall and serious, this inexplicable
great toy, this orphan, this strange guest of peace
which seemed to want peace, down to its wheeled feet.
However awful it is, we know the truth
by the joy it brings. And I woke in terror.

❖

Now, I've written you a scrip for Xanax
because your first two weeks on Zoloft
you're actually going to feel *more* tense, okay?
They *can* be addictive, so just when you need them.
Capisce? You'll probably have some ED,
so use the Viagra. And if you have more palpitations
we'll get you back on beta blockers, yah?

Dem bones, dem bones gonna walk aroun'
Dem bones, dem bones gonna walk aroun' [66]

We could do some Lunesta.
We could do some Ambien.

When we invent the drug that makes us
feel that God is present, will we
truly have created ourselves?

But let's deal with that anxiety first, okay, chief?

◈

---

[66] "Dem Dry Bones," a famous spiritual poem and song; the lyrics are based on the book of Ezekiel.

They had nothing to fear but fear itself.[67]
Fear of global financial collapse.
Fear of getting shot in the stairwell.
Fear of rising oceans and stronger storms.
Fear of losing their health insurance.
Fear of running out of oil.
Of not running out of oil.
Fear of a boredom so deep it throws up crude.
Fear of getting pregnant, of not getting pregnant.
Fear of the button. The pink slip. Blues in the rearviews.
Fear of the yawning pits they crossed in dreams.
Oh, history had made it clear:
They had nothing to fear but fear.

◆

---

[67] "[T]he only thing we have to fear is fear itself." Franklin D. Roosevelt, first inaugural address, 1933.

I swear to God someone is going to throw a harpoon
if I walk out of this changing room right now.
I mean, right? What is up with all these jeans
that make me look like a beached freakin' whale?
I'm not asking for God to come down from Mount Sinai—
Come on, that's a pretty good Professor Cole.
Just close one eye halfway like you can't take the pain:
"... *but sir, so what I plead is just—*
Why do sinners' ways prosper?"[68]
Let's find you a necklace to go with that shirt.
Something that draws the eyes into the cleavage.
My God, I would *kill* for breasts like yours.
I'm *not* even kidding—just look at these golf balls—

Mine, O thou lord of life, send my roots rain.[69]

❖

---

[68] Gerard Manley Hopkins, "Though Art Indeed Just, Lord."
[69] ibid.

When I reached Guantanamo the interrogation
went on for three or four hours. Then they left me
in an iron cage. Very cold.
I could not see anything or hear anything,
and I was like that for about two weeks.

Did they ever show you evidence?

Until I left they had absolutely no evidence to show.
They had something called, "secret evidence."

And how did they say they got it?

They say that, "We have secret evidence."[70]

❖

[70] Adel Hamad, interview, with Amy Goodman, 31 May 2008. Transcript from humanrights.
ucdavis.edu.

It just feels so *good* to talk, doesn't it?
To *say what's true*. To *get it all out*.
I sometimes think that's all our protests were.
I'm sure these kids care about the same things.
I'm sure there's a plan in each one of these backpacks
to save the world. And who knows, right?
We did eventually get out of Vietnam.
Most of us can still put our *pants* on in the morning.
So it's possible we won't just fry ourselves.
Do you know flowers at all? That white one there,
it might be some kind of viburnum, I'm not sure.
I'd like to have some for my rooftop garden.
God, Brooklyn! Please don't make me go back!
Look down this path right here. See how that arch
frames out the Tudor village just beyond it?
It's very beautiful—like nothing's been lost . . .
I've never said it wasn't beautiful.

◈

5

The Print of the Nails

"Space is open to us now; and our eagerness to share its meaning
is not governed by the efforts of others. We go into space because
whatever mankind must undertake, free men must fully share."
                    —John F. Kennedy, May 25,1961

                    "This' hard work,
        boss, wait' for The Word."
                    —John Berryman, Dream Song 10

A dusty light in October, a pained leaf-blower,
an Hispanic man with a leaf-blower on his back
like a sci-fi jet-pack. As though he stood
on the edge of a new frontier, of the 1960's.[71]
In the field beyond the house, some sheep
sheep-walk the hours,
considering the grass with studious mouths.
Winter may come, or it may not.
He lives in interesting times.

Space is open to him now.
His eagerness to share its meaning
is not governed by the efforts of others.[72]
The Price Chopper is open to him now.
The front of the bus is open to him now.
A million women on the Internet
are holding their legs open to him now.

He moves the leaves to the margins of the driveway,
squinting to see
what's right in front of him, always
New Jersey: land of farms and highways,
land of oxygen and SUVs.
Their land. His land.[73]

---

[71] "[W]e stand today on the edge of a New Frontier—the frontier of the 1960's." John F.
Kennedy, July 15, 1960.
[72] "Space is open to us now; and our eagerness to share its meaning is not governed by the
efforts of others." Kennedy, May 25, 1961.
[73] "This land is your land, this land is my land." Woody Guthrie, "This Land Is Your Land."

A light that is like a long reaching-after,
a light that has never been better.
The trees look digitally enhanced,
sharp with the shadows of far-off mountain ranges
or the moon on a clear night in Maine.

Beyond the trees, bold clouds ride low,
as clear and strange
as islands that have never seen a ship.

◈

I know it's a hassle, but I'm glad New Jersey
is finally doing something green.
Honey? When they're done with the lawn,
will you carry them to the curb?
We forgot last week so we have a ton.

Pile the bottles high at Lawrenceville.[74]

I know you're tired, hon.
Do you want to just watch a movie or something?
Do you want to just sit and read?

Do you want me to just be quiet and go away?

Shovel them under and let me work—

And the cars in the distance humming towards
New York or Philly, New York or Philly,
filled to all their empty seats with purpose—

They will get to the bottom of whatever it is.
They will break it apart, they will break it down.

They will put the pieces back together
to make some creature that maybe never walked,
but *could* have.

Do you see yonder cloud that's almost in shape of a camel?[75]

Senator, there is a lot to respond to in your statement.
I would respectfully disagree with your statement
that we're becoming more like our enemy.[76]

---

[74] "Pile the bodies high at Austerlitz and Waterloo. / Shovel them under and let me work— /
I am the grass; I cover all." Carl Sandburg, "Grass."

[75] Hamlet, to Polonius. *Hamlet*, III, ii, Shakespeare.

[76] Alberto Gonzales, Attorney General confirmation hearing before Congress, January 6, 2005.

The dusty light, the trees, their vines and branches
clinging into clouds—and roads unbroken,
roads that branch and branch,
like the aqueducts,
or the fissures in the vessels of the potter.[77]

Shovel them under and let me work—

◈

---

[77] "As the vessels of a potter shall they be broken to shivers." Revelation, 2:27.

Well, I think these things have CYCLES, Carson.
Traumas happen, and the earth recovers.
Ten thousand years ago, this was all under ice.
Bela, stop that! Come here! Come!
When I was growing up, it was THE COMMIES.
You'd be sitting in class in your knee-length checkered skirt
and the siren would go off and all of us
would DIVE under our desks because—*DUNH-dunh*—
THE COMMIES WERE ATTACKING! Joe McCarthy . . .
"I have here in my hand a list of names,"[78]
and everyone got hysterical. People lost their JOBS.
They went after all the FOLK SINGERS.
It was SILLY, Carson, it was JUST SILLY.
Oh, STOP that, Bela. Stop that RIGHT NOW.
When you were about ten years old, *Time* magazine
put a fried egg on its cover with something like,
"Cholesterol: The Silent Killer."
We were all supposed to eat margarine and Wonder Bread.
ALL the scientists said so. Well. GUESS WHAT.
People love to get hysterical.
That's what sells magazines, Carson.
And that's what sells all these PILLS everyone's taking.
Oxycontin? Lunesta? All these antidepressants?
Half my friends are walking around like zombies.
Oh WHAT is she into NOW. Bela!
You just can't resist those smells, now, can you.
No you CAN'T. No you CAN'T.
George, I think we should turn back now,
my hip is starting to do its thing.
I was sure it was getting better, I'm truly sorry.

❖

---

[78] "I have here in my hand a list of 205—a list of names that were made known to the Secretary of State as being members of the Communist Party and who nevertheless are still working and shaping policy in the State Department." Senator Joseph R. McCarthy, Feb. 9, 1950.

By the mass, and 'tis like a camel, indeed.

Methinks it is like a weasel.

It is *backed* like a weasel.

Or like a whale?

Very like a whale.[79]

◆

[79] op. cit., Shakespeare.

I would respectfully disagree with your statement
that we're becoming more like our enemy.
We are nothing like our enemy, Senator.
While we are struggling mightily to try to find out
what happened in Abu Ghraib, they are beheading people
like Danny Pearl and Nick Berg.
We are nothing like our enemy, Senator.[80]

These Arabs, Senator, slink around in their oil fields

while we are struggling mightily to find out
how so many could be beaten and waterboarded
in U.S.-run detention centers,
and how so many Iraqis could be dead
since U.S. troops invaded—Senator,

the fact is, we're still trying to find out
what happened in Dallas in '63,
in the days before Pearl Harbor, and in My Lai,
and in U.S.-backed coups in Chile, Malaysia,
Venezuela, Argentina, Haiti—

We're struggling, Senator, to try to find out
why even under the threat of destroying the planet
we just keep burning more gas and coal,
and driving more miles, and talking louder and louder

as though we lived in a dream, Senator,
and could shout ourselves awake at any moment,

like when we were sick as children, Senator,
burning with fever, the black gate swinging open—

Oh, Senator, how we are struggling!

---

[80] Alberto Gonzales, Attorney General confirmation hearing before Congress, January 6, 2005.

And all they can think to do
is behead Danny Pearl and Nick Berg.

❖

Two years, ten years, and passengers ask the conductor:[81]

Do you think these jeans make me look fat?

If Tom leaves from the same city at the same time as Jane,
traveling at a constant speed of 68 miles per hour—

Hey, what was the deal with the "spork," anyway?
Remember those?

What place is THIS? Where are we NOW—

the mountain rising beyond the edge of the ocean,
the joy bricked under the faces on the sidewalk,
the fire of the sun inside a rock

                         Only

there is fire inside this rock,
come in under the shadow of this viewing platform
and I will show you something different from either
a parafrag splitting a city block,
or a Panzer making rubble of a church[82]
I will show you something wicked cool, like,
Whoa! Dude!

Dude?

                      ◆

---

[81] "Two years, ten years, and passengers ask the conductor: / What place is this? / Where are we now?" op. cit., Sandburg.

[82] "Only / There is shadow under this red rock, / (Come in under the shadow of this red rock), / And I will show you something different from either / Your shadow at morning striding behind you / Or your shadow at evening rising to meet you; / I will show you fear in a handful of dust." T. S. Eliot, *The Waste Land*.

Two years, ten years

Twenty years.

Fifty years?

❖

Still wait' for the word, Boss.
Still wait' for the word.
I got the codes. I got the briefcase, Boss.
Hard work, Boss, haulin' roun' this briefcase.
Feels like a ton, Boss. Feels like the weight of the world.
And always bein' careful it don' go off, Boss.
But that's the thing been botherin' me, Boss.
First we work like dogs, we work like slaves
to make this thing—
and it's just so we can stay up all night frettin',
worryin' we gon' use the thing we made.
It's like these highways, Boss, it's like these jet planes—
we ain't supposed to use them either, *is* we—
not anymore, Boss, right?—these tractors
in the field, these furnaces, these power plants
that make these cities shine—*shine*, Boss,
just like your world shine, Boss, am I right?
We workin' since we had thumbs, Boss.
We workin' since we single cells, Boss,
tearin' ourself in *half* to make these cities—

◈

A dusty light in October, a light that was like
a long reaching after, the oceans and icecaps
still intact, the trees still stretching out,
still crowded thick at the suburb's edge, the clouds
of birds still reaching down to touch their tops.
And the way they walked in the streets was still intact,
the way they lined their cars up going and coming
and swore at each other with a kind of glee,
the way they sat by themselves whenever they wanted
and watched the snow settle down its desert
or listened to the wrenched chords right themselves,
or watched the Phillies right themselves and clinch,
and ate what they wanted and said what they wanted
at least to themselves, at least to what gods
they pictured as they wanted: they had
beat the Germans, the Japs and the Commies
and taught the Viet Cong a lesson;
they had beat Saddam and Milošević
and Bin Laden been runnin' from cave to cave—
they damn near had AIDS beat and cancer
was giving them options, giving them time;
crime was down and productivity
was soaring, the markets were showing signs
of steady improvement, key indicators
were hopeful, they'd found evidence
of water on the *moon*—

❖

It just hasn't really sunk in yet, you know?
I think it's gonna take a few days for this to sink in.
I mean, you wait this long for something like this—
twenty-eight years I've waited for this—
twenty-eight years—
I feel like I've watched nearly every goddamned pitch—
and something always goes wrong for us, you know?
I really just can't believe it, to be honest.
I mean, we can march down Broad in the parade,
and we can watch Charlie and Chase and J-Roll
holding up the trophy and all that,
but it still feels like I'm dreaming, you know?

Except I shall see in his hands the print of the nails,
and put my finger into the print of the nails,
and thrust my hand into his side—[83]

◈

[83] John, 20:25.

Now let's not get *too* carried away, son.
You ain't gotta take *that* many carts.
We gonna get 'em all put back in time.
They ain't gonna bother us none in Valley Stream.
Not after what happen Friday to Damour.[84]
We gonna be the *valued employee* today.
We what be making this company *thrive*.
And we not just be important 'cause of these here carts.
Oh, no. We be important as *individuals*.
Ha! You remember after 9/11,
how happy and friendly everybody was?
How we gonna send our money to them families?
How everybody suddenly *woke up to the possibility*
of living together like we was actually all here living together?
How people—even white people—
was lookin' you right in the *eye*?

◈

---

[84] Jdimytai Damour, a Walmart worker at Green Acres Mall in Valley Stream, New York, was
trampled to death by shoppers the day after Thanksgiving in 2008.

Okay. Okay. Let me try something else.
Look out this window, Chief.
Come on, just have a look.
See that woman with the shopping bag, on her cell?
You think she's discussing the end of civilization?
Okay, how about this guy—
looking into the window of the bookstore—
you think he's looking for something on nuclear winter?
Isn't it just a little more likely
DOCTOR OAKLEY TO THE TRAUMA CENTER DOCTOR
        OAKLEY
he's after a bedtime story for his daughter there—
something about honeybees or firemen?
How about all these people in front of the coffee shop,
chatting away, sipping their mochas or what have you.
They look pretty happy, don't they?
Now, who do you think needs the help here—them, or you?

❖

Ah, I don't know. I guess it's okay if she's there.
I'm over it, basically. Hello? Yah, okay.
It's just hard. I guess it just still feels—wrong.
Like it's not really over, even though I know it's over.
You live together for, what, two years?
You do everything together.
You get so fucking used to each other
it's like she's not even there. It's just—
life, you know? Easy. *Good.*
And then, *boom,* this door just slams in your face.
And you spend every goddam day for like a year
just trying to pry it back open.
You can't get out. Or in. Hell, I don't know.
I didn't even know there *was* a door.
I just . . . walked outside. And now it's like—
Marty? You there, buddy? Hello?

❖

The clouds are leaving and the sun stands over them.

The light is golden, the field is wide.
The parking lot is wide, the sky is wide—
wide is the road that leads to the Quaker Bridge Mall,[85]
the trees left sharp with shadows, sharp with light,
everything pulled out clean from the fire.

And who were the people who were questioning you there
and what were they asking you?

They were the Americans from the Army
and I would say, "I am just a normal worker,
and work and get my salary."[86]

I'm just a gigolo, and everywhere I go—[87]

I'm just a girl who cain't say no[88]

Thou art indeed JUST, Lord[89]

A handful of starlings tossed into the sky
to judge the wind for a fairway shot,
the oceans and icecaps still intact—

a light that is like a long reaching after,
a light that has never been better—

◈

---

[85] "For wide is the gate, and broad is the way, that leadeth to destruction." Matthew, 7:13.
[86] Adel Hamad, interview, with Amy Goodman, 31 May 2008. Transcript from humanrights.ucdavis.edu.
[87] "Just a Gigolo," Brammer, Caesar, Casucci, as adapted by David Lee Roth.
[88] "I Cain't Say No," Rodgers and Hammerstein.
[89] op. cit., Hopkins.

And what will be said about *them* when they are gone?
That they saw the sky for what it was?
The trees for what they were, the grass?
That they did better than their parents?
That they loved their children?
That they got up every morning and went to work?
That they were like children themselves, really,
borrowing things to play at being adults?
That look at these hieroglyphs—how cool is that?
That what they *felt* is ultimately more important
than whatever it was, exactly, they were doing?
That at least they left us these condominiums,
and countless gigs of research
and a flight path to the moon—
To the moon, Alice![90]
That most of what they did was actually *legal*?
That what is life for, if not to stroll campuses
and stand in chapels, under the huge stained glass?
That they had faith?
That given the crudeness of their instruments.
That, Dude! I found an arrowhead!
That all we can do is hope that they were happy.
That they were good people, damn it,
and if they gassed somebody, they must have had a reason.
That they *were* good people.
That they were free?
That there goes one of them now! Oh—
no, it's just black ink shining bright.[91]
That did they really die of pseudoscience?
That it's obvious to *us*, of course.
That are you sure you haven't combined

---

[90] "One of these days—Pow! Right in the kisser! One of these days, Alice, straight to the moc
Ralph threatening his wife, Alice, on the hit TV show *The Honeymooners.*
[91] "O none, unless this miracle have might, / That in black ink my love may still shine brig
Shakespeare, Sonnet 65.

the actions of one creature
with the conscience of another?
That who are we to judge them, we of the future,
who do not yet even know who we really are?

◈

I should like to object to the indictment.
I should like to say that in my opinion,

as far as   THE AMERICANS   are concerned,

the indictment does not conform to Article VII.
I can explain that.[92]

❖

---

[92] "I should like to object to the indictment. I should like to say that in my opinion, as far as Schaefer is concerned, the indictment does not conform to Article VII. I can explain that." Dr. Pelckmann, defense attorney for Konrad Wilhelm Schaefer, standing trial at the Nuremberg Trials for using Jews in human experiments.

Can you help me out with these cans first?
Honey?
Are you too busy staring out the window right now?
What are we doing? I mean, *what are we doing?*

Is this your way of ending things?
Is that what you want?
I have no idea anymore.

I want to go walking the path by the harbor.

I know we have problems—do you think I don't know we have
        problems?
But people *work* on their problems, honey.
They *talk* to each other. We have to talk.
We have to be *able* to talk. In the real world—
Does that even sound *familiar?*

where the sun rakes its fingers in through the thin trees
and the ocean has filled every gap in their ribs,
every gap in the trunks where the death could blow through
and the harbor is held by your own arms around it
and there stand the boats that have been there forever—
their masts are all bare and they're all through with wind—
and you could sit and watch while the sun makes them shadows
and you could just keep walking away through the dream
but wherever you go you will be in this place

◈

Well, Little Pea, we *have* gone there.
Astronauts went there. They took some pictures.
They got some rocks. One of them hit a golf ball.
But no one could *live* on the moon, sweetie.
I know it looks nice from down here—
but there's not any air to breathe, for one thing.
And there aren't any plants, or trees, or animals,
or really any of the things you love.
It's really just a big rock, sweetie.
It's just a big, empty rock up there, floating around.

❖

The clouds are leaving and the sun stands over them.
They sail and glimmer, drifting by.
Here is a flame-legged spirit, dissolving.
It is backed like a flame-legged spirit . . .
And here go two lovers, one's feathery hands
firmly on the other's airy shoulders.

They are melting together, gliding backwards,
back to the town where their real life can begin.

STILL WAIT' FOR THE WORD, BOSS.

And here is a walrus, and here a woolly mammoth.
And here the bones have been put together
to make some creature that never walked—but *could* have.

WE READY WHEN YOU IS, BOSS.

Wert thou my enemy, O thou my friend.[93]

Honey can you hear me in there, honey?

*My client cannot tell
what the nature of his participation
is supposed to have been.*[94]

A ragged strand of geese, each tugging singly
at his private burden, shouts into the sky:
Honk-ick!—call. *Honk-ick!*—response.

---

[93] op. cit., Hopkins.
[94] op. cit., Pelckmann.

WE WAITIN', BOSS.

Gentile or Jew[95]

We are on the line 157 337.
We will repeat this message.
We will repeat this on 6210 kilocycles.[96]

❖ ❖ ❖

[95] "Gentile or Jew / O you who turn the wheel and look to windward, / Consider Phlebas, who was once handsome and tall as you." T. S. Eliot, *The Waste Land.*
[96] Amelia Earhart's last received transmission.

Acknowledgments

Parts 1 and 5, as "The Last Part of the Night" and "Waitin' for the Word," appeared in *At Length*; Part 2, as "The Turns They Have Taken," in *Post Road*; Part 3, as "The Other Lane," in *Epoch*; Part 4, "Secret Evidence," appeared in *The Literary Review*; and the monologue beginning "And what will be said about them when they are gone?" appeared in *32 Poems*.

I am grateful to so many friends for their help with this manuscript, especially Kristen Tracy, James Richardson, Whitney Terrell, Porter Fox, Michael Morse, Alex Halberstadt, Kate Macko, Weslea Sidon, John Rosenwald, and (*il miglior fabbro*) Jeffrey Thomson.

◈

About the Author

Christian Barter's first book of poems, *The Singers I Prefer,* was a finalist for the Lenore Marshall Prize, and his second collection, *In Someone Else's House,* was the winner of a 2014 Maine Literary Award. His poetry has appeared in *Ploughshares, Georgia Review, North American Review, The American Scholar,* and other magazines, and has been featured on *Poetry Daily, Verse Daily, The PBS Newshour,* and *The Writer's Almanac.* He has received residency fellowships from Yaddo and The MacDowell Colony, and he was a Hodder Fellow in Creative Writing at Princeton University. He is a supervisor of the trail crew at Acadia National Park in Bar Harbor, Maine, where he is currently serving as Poet Laureate of Acadia.

❖

BOA Editions, Ltd.
American Poets Continuum Series

Colophon

The Isabella Gardner Poetry Award is given biennially to a poet in mid-career with a new book of exceptional merit. Poet, actress, and associate editor of *Poetry* magazine, Isabella Gardner (1915–1981) published five celebrated collections of poetry, was three times nominated for the National Book Award, and was the first recipient of the New York State Walt Whitman Citation of Merit for Poetry. She championed the work of young and gifted poets, helping many of them to find publication.

BOA Editions, Ltd., a not-for-profit publisher of poetry and other literary works, fosters readership and appreciation of contemporary literature. By identifying, cultivating, and publishing both new and established poets and selecting authors of unique literary talent, BOA brings high-quality literature to the public. Support for this effort comes from the sale of its publications, grant funding, and private donations.

❖ ❖ ❖

The publication of this book is made possible, in part, by the support of the following patrons:

Anonymous
Gwen & Gary Conners
Steven O. Russell & Phyllis Rifkin-Russell

and the kind sponsorship of the following individuals:

Dr. James & Ann Burk, *in memory of Jack Sheehan*
Susan Burke & Bill Leonardi, *in honor of Boo Poulin*
Christopher & DeAnna Cebula
Jere Fletcher
Peg Heminway, *in honor of Grant Holcomb*
Sandi Henschel
X.J. & Dorothy M. Kennedy
Boo Poulin
Deborah Ronnen & Sherman Levey
Steven O. Russell & Phyllis Rifkin-Russell
Sue Stewart, *in memory of Stephen L. Raymond*
Michael Waters & Mihaela Moscaliuc

Printed in the USA
CPSIA information can be obtained
at www.ICGtesting.com
JSHW080003150824
68134JS00021B/2247